Wild Flowers

Bob Press

Illustrated by
Josephine Martin

Piccolo
A Piper Book

Contents

Introduction	3
What to Look For	4
Picking and Preserving Flowers	10
Where to Go From Here	11
IDENTIFICATION SECTION	
Woods and Hedgerows	12
Fields, Meadows and Marshes	22
Wasteground	31
The Seaside	38
Heaths and Moors	42
Index	48

Illustrated by Josephine Martin/
The Garden Studio

Edited by Angela Royston

Introduction

The type of place where a flower grows is called its habitat. Similar habitats usually have the same flowers growing there. But if one habitat is slightly different to another then the flowers growing there will be different. For example you will find some flowers in a beech wood that do not grow in an oak wood. The type of soil in the habitat is very important too. Grassy habitats with a chalk soil have different flowers to grassy places with a clay soil.

To help you name them, the flowers in this book have been grouped according to the habitat in which you are most likely to find them. For each flower described, there are spaces for you to record the date, place and habitat where you first saw it. Some flowers can grow happily in different places so you will sometimes find the same flowers in different habitats.

This book shows the flowers you are most likely to find. You may know some of them already, especially those which grow around your home. Some of them are probably 'weeds', that is plants which can grown almost anywhere. When you visit other areas see how the plants differ from those around your home.

You need very little equipment to collect and name flowers. A notebook and pencil are useful for making sketches of leaves and flowers. Write down any feature which can help you to name the flower later. A magnifying glass is useful for looking at small flowers. If you are collecting flowers take a plastic bag to put them in. They will stay fresh until you get home. Remember, never collect too many.

If you would like to grow wild flowers in your garden you can buy packets of wild flower seeds. In this way you can pick as many of them as you like.

What to Look For

Learn the different parts of a flower. They are shown in the drawing on the next page. Most parts of a flower can give some clues to what that flower is. The most important are the petals. Note their number, shape and arrangement. The colour of the petals is also very useful, but sometimes the same flowers can have petals of different colours. The shape and colour of the sepals, leaves and fruits and the way these parts are arranged are also important.

Make a note of the habitat where the flower is growing. The flowers in this book are arranged by habitat to help you identify them. The time of year when the flower is open is also helpful. Most flowers only open during a particular season, some in spring, some in early summer and so on.

GLOSSARY
Anther Part of the stamen that produces pollen.
Bristly Covered with stiff hairs.
Clock A head of downy seeds.
Colony Place where many plants grow together.
Drift-line Line of litter washed up by the tide.
Evergreen Plant which keeps its leaves all year.
Eye Coloured circle in the centre of a flower.
Fleshy Swollen and pulpy.
Leaf-blade The broad, flat part of a leaf.
Leaflet One of several parts which make up one leaf.
Rosette Cluster of leaves surrounding the base of a stem.
Runner Stem which grows along the ground and puts down roots.
Spike A long, thin cluster of flowers.
Spur A tube which sticks out from the back of the flower.
Tendril Slender stalk which twists around things.
Vein One of the lines on a leaf.
Whorl A ring of parts such as leaves.

THE PARTS OF A FLOWER

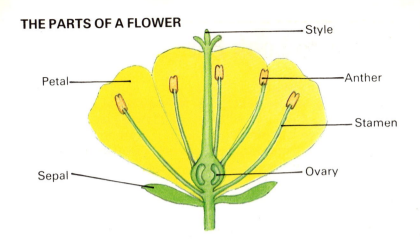

HOW FLOWERS REPRODUCE

Flowers have male parts (stamens) and female parts (styles and ovaries). The male parts produce a yellow powder called pollen. When pollen from the stamens of one flower is transferred to the style of another flower of the same kind, it causes seeds to form inside the ovary. This transfer of pollen is called pollination. Two ways in which pollen is transferred are by insects and by wind.

Some flowers are brightly coloured and produce nectar to attract insects such as bees. Pollen from the stamens is brushed onto the bee. When the bee visits other flowers, this pollen sticks to their styles.

Some flowers release lots of pollen into the air. The wind blows it onto the styles of other flowers. These flowers do not need to attract insects. They produce no nectar and are usually small and green.

HOW FLOWERS GROW

Many flowers have distinctive shapes or ways of growing. The stem can have many branches or only a few. Look for runners or creeping stems which spread out from the main stem and put down roots.

SHAPES OF PETALS AND HOW THEY GROW

Always count the number of petals and look at their shape and colour. Sometimes they are joined

Four entire petals

Five notched petals

FLOWER-HEADS

The flowers can be arranged in different ways. They may be single or grouped together in heads or spikes. Flower-heads can be different shapes. Spikes can have all the flowers hanging on one side.

Single flower

Spike with all the flowers on one side

Umbrella-shaped head

Flat head

together. Look for a spur at the back of the petals.

Sometimes the sepals are coloured like the petals.

Petals joined

Petals with spur

SHAPES OF LEAVES

Look at the overall shape of the leaf. Some leaves are divided into separate leaflets. Look at the edges of the leaf. Does it have teeth or spines? Some leaves are very thin, others are thick and fleshy.

KINDS OF FRUIT

The fruit or seed-pod can be a useful clue to help you name a flower. Learn to recognize the fruits of flowers you know already. Then you can identify the flower even when the petals have faded. Remember that some fruits are poisonous.

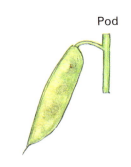

HOW LEAVES GROW

The way leaves grow is important. Examine the stem carefully, especially at the bottom. The leaves that grow there are often a different shape or are grouped differently to the leaves higher up the stem.

Rosette

Whorls

Pairs

Alternate

Capsule

Berry

Clock

Picking and Preserving Flowers

New plants grow from seeds. The seeds only form if the flowers are left to be pollinated. Some plants have become rare because too many of their flowers were picked early, before the seeds formed. In 1975 a law was passed to protect some of our rarest flowers from being picked at all.

If you do pick plants, follow these rules. Only pick flowers which are very common, like buttercups or campions. Never pick all the flowers – leave some to form seeds. Don't pick any flower which you do not know – it might be rare. Never pick any rare flower. Some plants like bluebells and poppies wither and die very soon after being picked, even if you put them in water. Please don't pick them.

Never dig up the roots of any wild flower; it is against the law. Try not to damage flowers by trampling on or around them. This breaks the stems and hardens the ground so that seeds cannot grow in it.

PRESERVING FLOWERS

If you want to keep any of the common wild flowers which you have collected, you can preserve them. The easiest way to do this is to press them. Place the flower between two sheets of blotting paper or thick newspaper. Put these between two sheets of cardboard and place a heavy weight, such as a large book, on top. Or you can buy a special plant press. Leave the flower under the book or in the press until it is completely dry.

Afterwards you can stick it to a piece of paper and write on it the date and place where you found it.

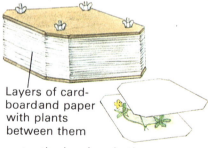

Layers of cardboard and paper with plants between them

Where to Go From Here

When you have learned to recognize the more common flowers, there are several societies which you can join. If you write to any of them, enclose a stamped addressed envelope.

Wild Life Youth Service, Wallington, Surrey. This group has projects and a quarterly newsletter.

Natural History Societies. You can get the address of your local society from The Council for Nature, The Zoological Gardens, Regents Park, London NW1 4RY. The societies deal with animals as well as plants.

The Wild Flower Society, c/o Harvest House, 62 London Road, Reading. This society deals only with wild flowers and will help you identify any that you cannot name for yourself.

The British Naturalist Association, Mrs K. L. Butcher, Boynes Wood Road, Four Marks, Alston, Hants and your local branch of the **County Naturalist Trust** are also good societies to join.

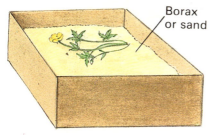
Borax or sand

Make a note of the habitat and any other plants which were growing nearby.

You can also preserve flowers by drying them in borax powder or silica gel. Put a layer of borax powder or silica gel in the bottom of a box. Lay the flower on top and carefully cover with more borax powder or silica gel. Leave it until the flower is completely dry and feels papery. Dried in this way, the flower will keep its shape.

Some parts of a plant like the seed-heads of cotton grass and poppy capsules can be picked ready-dried by the sun and wind. They do not need any other treatment to preserve them.

Woods and Hedgerows

All plants need some sunlight, but the leaves of woodland trees can prevent sunlight from reaching the ground. Some plants can survive in shade and grow beneath the trees. Others flower in the spring before the trees are leafy enough to block out the sun. You will find a greater variety of plants along the edges of woods and beside the paths through the trees where there is more light. Most flowers that grow in the woods like to have some shade.

Hedgerows are a good place for many kinds of flowers to grow. Many are very old and have been left undisturbed for a long time. Hedges provide a barrier against the wind and shelter the flowers growing there. The branches of the hedge provide a framework for climbing plants to cling to. Hedgerows also provide shade for those plants which like it, so look for woodland plants here too.

DOG'S MERCURY
A hairy, upright plant with pairs of toothed leaves. Tiny green flowers form slender spikes. Look for the male and female flowers which grow on separate plants. Forms large patches in shady places. The whole plant has a strong, unpleasant smell and is **poisonous**.
Height: Up to 40 cm
Flowers: February–April

DATE_____

PLACE_____

HABITAT_____

WOOD ANEMONE
The stem has a ring of three leaves about one third of the way down. Each leaf is divided into three leaflets. The white flowers have five to nine petal-like sepals. Look for pink streaks on the back of them. Forms large colonies in woods. Also called wind flower or granny's nightcap.
Height: 6 to 30 cm
Flowers: March–May

DATE_____

PLACE_____

HABITAT_____

RAMSONS
The leaves are broad and bright green. Each stem carries a cluster of white star-shaped flowers with slender stalks. Ramsons grows in the shady parts of old woods. Where many plants grow together, the air smells strongly of garlic.
Height: Up to 45 cm
Flowers: April–August

DATE_____

PLACE_____

HABITAT_____

BLUEBELL

Bluebells carpet the ground in open woods. The drooping, bell-shaped flowers all hang on one side of the stem. Sometimes the flowers are pink or white. Clusters of long, strap-shaped leaves surround each stem. Bluebells do not like too much shade so look for them in hedgerows too.
Height: 20–50 cm
Flowers: April–June

DATE_____

PLACE_____

HABITAT_____

LORDS AND LADIES

The flower-head is a pale green hood wrapped around a purple spike. It smells of rotten meat to attract flies which pollinate the flowers. The glossy leaves are broad and shaped like arrow-heads. Look for dark spots on the leaves. After flowering, clusters of **poisonous** berries form.
Height: 30–45 cm
Flowers: April–May

DATE_____

PLACE_____

HABITAT_____

PRIMROSE

The pale yellow flowers have a darker 'eye' in the middle. Several flowers grow from the centre of a rosette of leaves. Each wrinkled leaf is hairy underneath. Look for primroses in hedgerows and on sunny banks as well as in open woods.
Height: up to 15 cm
Flowers: March–May

DATE_____

PLACE_____

HABITAT_____

LESSER CELANDINE

The bright yellow flowers have eight to twelve petals and three green sepals. The petals fade to white as they get older. The leaves are heart-shaped and glossy green. They have long stalks. Look for lesser celandines in the damp parts of shady places.
Height: 6–15 cm
Flowers: March–May

DATE_____

PLACE_____

HABITAT_____

IVY

The shiny, dark green leaves have five lobes and a pattern of pale veins. Clusters of green flowers attract wasps in the autumn. Look for ivy climbing up trees or walls by means of its string-like roots. The black berries are **poisonous**.
Height: Up to 30 metres
Flowers: September–November

DATE_____

PLACE_____

HABITAT_____

BLACKBERRY

Long, prickly stems sprawl in woods and hedgerows. They may form large patches. The leaves are divided into three or five leaflets. The flowers may be white or pink. The berries are black when ripe and can be eaten. Look for new plants forming where the stems have touched the ground and taken root.
Height: Up to 90 cm
Flowers: May–September

DATE_____

PLACE_____

HABITAT_____

FOXGLOVE

The petals of each flower are joined together to form a bell-shaped tube. Look for the black spots on the inside of the petal tube. They attract and guide bees to the mouth of the flower. The large oval leaves are soft and hairy. The plant is **poisonous**, and it is said to be unlucky to pick them.
Height: 60–150 cm
Flowers: June–August

DATE_____

PLACE_____

HABITAT_____

HERB ROBERT

The leaves are lobed and deeply toothed. Both the stems and the leaves are sometimes coloured red and smell unpleasant. The flowers have five pink petals and droop at night or in bad weather. Look for the pointed fruit which is supposed to look like a crane's bill.
Height: 10–50 cm
Flowers: May–September

DATE_____

PLACE_____

HABITAT_____

VETCHES

Several different kinds of vetch grow along hedgerows. They climb or scramble among other plants. You can tell three of the common ones apart by looking carefully at the flowers and at the leaves which are divided into leaflets.

Tufted vetch
Many flowers in each cluster. The leaf has a branched tendril at the tip.
Height: 60–200 cm
Flowers: June–August

DATE_____

PLACE_____

Bitter vetch
Few flowers in each cluster. The leaf has a narrow leaflet at the tip. There are no tendrils.
Height: 15–40 cm
Flowers: April–July

Bush vetch
Few flowers in each cluster. The leaf has a branched tendril at the tip.
Height: 30–100 cm
Flowers: May–August

DATE_____ DATE_____

PLACE_____ PLACE_____

SWEET VIOLET
This is the only kind of violet with sweet-scented flowers. They are usually blue or violet but you can find white flowers too. Look for the pale coloured spur at the back of the petals. Violets grow in clumps from one point and have many heart-shaped leaves.
Height: 1–6 cm
Flowers: January–April

DATE_____

PLACE_____

HABITAT_____

RED CAMPION
Two common kinds of campion grow in hedgerows. Red campion has red or pink flowers. White campion has only white flowers. They both have notched petals. Look for the sepals which are joined into a sticky tube. The stems are hairy and sticky too.
Height: 30–90 cm
Flowers: May–June

DATE_____

PLACE_____

HABITAT_____

GREATER STITCHWORT

Very narrow, pointed leaves form pairs up the stem. Look for rough edges on the leaves and stems. The flowers have green sepals and white, split petals. The stems of greater stitchwort snap easily so be careful not to break them. It is sometimes called snapjack or star of Bethlehem.
Height: 15–60 cm
Flowers: April–June

DATE_____

PLACE_____

HABITAT_____

COW PARSLEY

The ribbed stems are tall and hollow. The small, white flowers form umbrella-shaped heads. Look for the flowers at the edge of each head. They have one petal much larger than the others. Cow parsley is one of the commonest plants that you can find along roadside hedges.
Height: 60–120 cm
Flowers: April–June

DATE_____

PLACE_____

HABITAT_____

GARLIC MUSTARD

Also called Jack-by-the-hedge. White flowers form clusters at the tops of the stems. Look for the four petals which form the shape of a cross. The triangular or heart-shaped leaves have toothed edges and smell of garlic. Garlic mustard grows in shady parts of hedgerows.
Height: 20–120 cm
Flowers: April–June

DATE_____

PLACE_____

HABITAT_____

TRAVELLER'S JOY

Also called old man's beard because of its white, feathery fruits. Look for the twisting leaf stalks which help the plant to climb high up bushes and trees. Sprays of white flowers decorate the hedgerows in summer. An old name for this flower is boy's bacca.
Height: up to 30 metres
Flowers: July–August

DATE_____

PLACE_____

HABITAT_____

Fields, Meadows and Marshes

Different kinds of flowers grow in different kinds of field. Grassy fields and meadows are used for grazing animals and growing hay. The flowers growing there must avoid being cut or eaten by cattle, sheep and even wild rabbits. Daisies have low-growing leaves which will not be bitten off. Thistles have prickly stems and leaves. Meadowsweet and buttercups have a bitter taste.

Where meadows are very wet for all or part of the year you will find marsh plants. There are more kinds of flowers here than in the dry fields. They are often taller too, because the soil is richer and grazing animals cannot reach them. When wet meadows are drained marsh flowers can no longer grow. They are then gradually replaced by flowers from the drier fields.

RIBWORT
The leaves form a rosette. Each leaf blade has three, four or five veins running down it. The tiny flowers are packed into a club-shaped head. White anthers stick out from the head. This plant is sometimes called fighting cocks or cocks and hens.
Height: up to 45 cm
Flowers: April–August

DATE_____

PLACE_____

HABITAT_____

HARDHEADS
A bushy plant with many tough stems. Hardheads looks like a thistle but there are no spines or prickles. Look for the dark, knob-shaped flowers which grow at the tips of the stems. It also grows on cliffs and on the sides of roads. It is also known as lesser knapweed.
Height: 30–60 cm
Flowers: June–September

DATE_____

PLACE_____

HABITAT_____

FIELD SCABIOUS
Field scabious has round flat heads of blue or lilac flowers. Look carefully at the flowers. Those at the edge of the head are much larger than the middle flowers. The lobed leaves are dull green. It grows in dry fields and grassy places, and is also known as gypsy rose.
Height: 25–100 cm
Flowers: July–September

DATE_____

PLACE_____

HABITAT_____

DANDELION
The flat, bright yellow flowers grow on hollow stalks. Sticky white juice oozes from the end of the stalks when they are picked. Look for the 'clocks' of seeds. Dandelions grow in lawns and on waste ground as well as in fields.
Height: 5–30 cm
Flowers: March–October

DATE_____

PLACE_____

HABITAT_____

DAISY
Daisies grow in almost any field where the grass is short. The flowers have white or pink petals around a yellow centre. They close up at night or in dull weather. Look for the flat rosettes of spoon-shaped leaves.
Height: 3–20 cm
Flowers: August–September

DATE_____

PLACE_____

HABITAT_____

BUTTERCUPS

Different kinds of buttercup grow in different kinds of grassland. You can recognize them by looking carefully at the leaves and sepals.

Bulbous buttercup
This buttercup is found in dry fields. Each leaf has a stalked middle lobe. Unlike the other two, the sepals curve away from the petals.
Height: 30–90 cm
Flowers: March–June

DATE _____

PLACE _____

Meadow buttercup
This buttercup is found in damp fields. The lobes of the leaves do not have stalks.
Height: 30–90 cm
Flowers: May onwards

Creeping buttercup
This buttercup grows in wet fields and meadows. The middle lobe of each leaf has a stalk.
Height: 5–50 cm
Flowers: May–September

DATE_____

PLACE_____

DATE_____

PLACE_____

RAGGED ROBIN

The ragged-looking petals have given this plant its name. The flowers are usually pink but look out for plants with white flowers. The upright stems have pairs of leaves and grow in wet meadows and marshes. It is also called ragged Jack or Robin Hood.
Height: 30–75 cm
Flowers: May–June

DATE

PLACE

HABITAT

CURLED DOCK

Docks are very common plants. The long leaves have very wavy edges and often turn red in autumn. Dock leaves are a cure for nettle stings. The flower spikes have many tiny green flowers. Look for the red and green fruits which appear after the flowers.
Height: 50–100 cm
Flowers: June–October

DATE

PLACE

HABITAT

WHITE CLOVER

Clover leaves are divided into three leaflets. Look for the white horseshoe-shaped band on each one. Lucky four-leaved clover is very rare. Red clover looks like white clover except for the colour of the flowers.
Height: up to 50 cm
Flowers: June–September

DATE_____

PLACE_____

HABITAT_____

BUGLE

The leaves of bugle can be dark glossy green or bronze. The stem carries pairs of leaves and rings of blue flowers. Look for runners which spread out from the flowering stems. Bugle grows in damp woods as well as in fields.
Height: 10–30 cm
Flowers: May–July

DATE_____

PLACE_____

HABITAT_____

MARSH MARIGOLD
Marsh marigold looks like a very large buttercup and is sometimes called a kingcup. Look for the petals which are bright yellow on the inside and greenish on the outside. The glossy leaves are heart-shaped.
Height: 30–60 cm
Flowers: March–July

DATE_____

PLACE_____

HABITAT_____

MEADOWSWEET
The cream-coloured flower heads contain many tiny, sweet-smelling flowers. The leaves are divided into leaflets. Look for pairs of very small leaflets between the larger ones. Meadowsweet sometimes forms large colonies in wet meadows and marshes. It is also called bittersweet.
Height: 60–120 cm
Flowers: June–August

DATE_____

PLACE_____

HABITAT_____

CUCKOO FLOWER

The leaves of cuckoo flower are divided into leaflets. The flowers are usually lilac but sometimes they are white. **Look for the narrow seed-pods.** When they are ripe they explode, scattering the seeds a long way from the plant. This flower is also known as lady's smock.
Height: 15–60 cm
Flowers: April–June

DATE_____

PLACE_____

HABITAT_____

FRAGRANT ORCHID

Fragrant orchid is difficult to find before the flowers open. The leaves are narrow and grass-like. The flowers smell strongly of cloves and attract moths to pollinate them. Look for the long spur at the back of each flower.
Height: 15–40 cm
Flowers: June–August

DATE_____

PLACE_____

HABITAT_____

WELTED THISTLE

The whole plant is spiny and prickly. Look for the spiny wing which runs all the way down the stem. The groups of purple flowers attract many bees, flies and butterflies. This thistle grows in damp grassy places and by streams.
Height: 30–120 cm
Flowers: June–August

DATE_____

PLACE_____

HABITAT_____

TUFTED FORGET-ME-NOT

There are several kinds of forget-me-not. This one grows in marshes and beside water. The flower spikes are coiled at first, then unwind as the flowers open. Look for the yellow eye in the centre of each flower. Sometimes the flowers are pink or white but they always have a yellow eye.
Height: 20–40 cm
Flowers: May–August

DATE_____

PLACE_____

HABITAT_____

Wasteground

Waste places are areas where the soil has been disturbed and left bare. They are often covered with litter or bricks and stones. Waste places can be any forgotten corner of land, in towns as well as in the countryside. Building sites, railway sidings and rubbish dumps are all examples of waste places.

The first plants to appear in waste places are those which can take root and grow quickly, such as chickweed and poppies. Later, other plants such as nettles move in. They may take over completely from the first plants.

Many of the plants which grow in waste places are well-known weeds. You can also find them in gardens and ploughed fields. The freshly dug soil provides ideal conditions for them to grow.

POPPY
Poppies have large, bright red flowers. Each flower only lasts for one day. Look for the seed-pods shaped like pepper-pots. Long-headed poppy has longer, narrower pods than field poppy.
Height: 20–60 cm
Flowers: May–October

DATE_____

PLACE_____

HABITAT_____

COMMON FIELD-SPEEDWELL

The spreading stems have pairs of toothed, pale green leaves. A long slender flower stalk grows from the base of each leaf stalk. The flowers are bright blue. Look for the lowest petal which is smaller and paler than the others. Look for it in ploughed fields and cornfields.
Height: 10–40 cm
Flowers: all year round

DATE_____

PLACE_____

HABITAT_____

SCARLET PIMPERNEL

Spreading stems grow along the ground. The flowers are usually scarlet but you may find plants which have blue flowers. You can tell the time by the flowers. They close at 3 o'clock in the afternoon, or earlier if the weather is wet or dull. It is also known **as poor man's weather-glass.**
Height: 5–30 cm
Flowers: May–August

DATE_____

PLACE_____

HABITAT_____

CHICKWEED

This is one of the first plants to appear on bare ground. The trailing stems may form mats. The white flowers are star-shaped. Look for the five white petals. Each one is deeply split so that it looks like two petals.
Height: 5–35 cm
Flowers: all year round

DATE_____

PLACE_____

HABITAT_____

SHEPHERD'S PURSE

Upright stems carry spikes of tiny white flowers. Each flower has four petals forming the shape of a cross. Look for the heart-shaped seed-pods. When they are picked they break open and the seeds spill out like coins from a purse. Also called mother's heart.
Height: 7–45 cm
Flowers: all year round

DATE_____

PLACE_____

HABITAT_____

DAISIES
These three plants are all common in waste places, and they have similar-looking flowers. To tell them apart, look at the shape of the leaves and the number of flowers on the stems.

Scentless mayweed
The leaves are divided into very narrow lobes. Each stem has a single flower.
Height: 15–60 cm
Flowers: July–September

DATE_____

PLACE_____

Scentless mayweed   Ox-eye daisy

NETTLES AND DEAD-NETTLES
Nettles and dead-nettles look alike and often grow together. They have upright stems and pairs of toothed, wrinkled leaves. Look for the flowers of each plant.

Nettle
Drooping clusters of tiny green flowers grow from the base of each leaf stalk. The leaves sting.
Height: up to 150 cm
Flowers: May–September

DATE_____

PLACE_____

Nettle

Feverfew

Ox-eye daisy
The leaves are deeply toothed. Each stem has a single flower.
Height: 20–60 cm
Flowers: July–September

Feverfew
The leaves are divided into toothed lobes. Each stem has more than one flower.
Height: 25–60 cm
Flowers: July–August

DATE_____

PLACE_____

DATE_____

PLACE_____

White dead-nettle   Red dead-nettle

White dead-nettle
A ring of large white flowers grows above each pair of leaves.
Height: 20–60 cm
Flowers: May–December

Red dead-nettle
Looks like white dead-nettle but has red or purple flowers.
Height: 10–45 cm
Flowers: March–October

DATE_____

PLACE_____

DATE_____

PLACE_____

ROSEBAY WILLOWHERB
A tall plant with narrow leaves and long spikes of pink flowers. Look for the narrow, purple sepals behind the broad petals. Rosebay willowherb can cover large areas of waste ground. The seed-pods are full of feathery seeds. It is also known as fire weed.
Height: up to 120 cm
Flowers: June–September

DATE_____

PLACE_____

HABITAT_____

BINDWEED
Climbs by twisting its stems around other plants. Sometimes the stems sprawl along the ground. The leaves are arrowhead-shaped. The pretty pink flowers are funnel-shaped. Look for white stripes on the inside of the funnel. It is also called Devil's guts.
Height: 20–75 cm
Flowers: June–September

DATE_____

PLACE_____

HABITAT_____

GOOSEGRASS

Whorls of narrow leaves ring the stem. Tiny prickles on the stems and leaves make them feel rough and sticky to touch. Look for the round fruits. They are covered in hooked spines and stick to passing animals or birds. Goosegrass is also known as sticky Willy and cleavers.
Height: 15–120 cm
Flowers: June–August

DATE_____

PLACE_____

HABITAT_____

CREEPING THISTLE

A tall plant with very prickly leaves. The purple flowers are prickly too. Large clumps of creeping thistle attract butterflies in summer. The flowers produce many downy seeds which are blown away by the wind.
Height: 30–150 cm
Flowers: July–September

DATE_____

PLACE_____

HABITAT_____

The Seaside

Cliffs, sand dunes and shingle beaches are dry places because rainwater drains away very quickly. Seaside plants need to store water and stop it from escaping. Some have thick, fleshy leaves covered with a waxy coat. Others roll up their leaves in sunny weather or have a thick coat of hairs to stop the leaves from drying out.

Most seaside plants have roots which grow deep to find water. Deep roots also help to anchor cliff plants against strong winds, and to anchor shingle plants which grow in constantly shifting pebbles.

Few plants can grow in salty ground. Further away from the sea the ground gets less salty by stages. More types of plants are able to survive at each stage, or zone. Look for these zones of plants along the shore.

VIPER'S BUGLOSS
A very bristly plant. Most of the leaves grow in a rosette at the base of the stem. The flowers grow in coiled sprays. Look for the pink buds which turn blue as the flowers open. Grows on dunes and cliffs.
Height: 30–90 cm
Flowers: June–September

DATE

PLACE

HABITAT

HORNED POPPY
The large, bright yellow flowers of horned poppy can be seen from a distance. It has deep, strong roots which anchor it in shingle. The blue-grey leaves are lobed and very tough. Look for the very long, thin seed-pods. Horned poppy is **poisonous**.
Height: 30–90 cm
Flowers: June–October

DATE_____

PLACE_____

HABITAT_____

COMMON RAGWORT
The dark green leaves are deeply divided. Stems are branched with yellow flowers at the tips. The seed-heads are like miniature dandelion clocks. A common weed. Look for it on waste ground as well as on the seashore. It is also called ragweed.
Height: 30–120 cm
Flowers: June–October

DATE_____

PLACE_____

HABITAT_____

SEA ROCKET

The sprawling stems of sea rocket grow along the drift-line at the top of beaches. Look for the lobed leaves which are thick and fleshy. Clusters of pink flowers with four petals grow at the tips of the stems. The fruits can float and are spread by the tide.
Height: 15–30 cm
Flowers: June–August

DATE_____

PLACE_____

HABITAT_____

SEA HOLLY

A bushy plant with stiff stems. The tough, blue-grey leaves are very spiny and are covered with a waxy coat. Look for the prickly blue flower-heads. Sea holly often covers large patches of sand or shingle.
Height: 30–90 cm
Flowers: July–August

DATE_____

PLACE_____

HABITAT_____

THRIFT

Thrift grows on rocks and cliffs. The flowers are crowded into heads at the tips of long stalks. Evergreen rosettes of narrow, grass-like leaves are blue-green and fleshy. Look beneath the leaves for the thick, woody stem. It is also known as seapink.
Height: up to 15 cm
Flowers: April–August

DATE_____

PLACE_____

HABITAT_____

ROCK SAMPHIRE

The umbrella-shaped flower-heads have many tiny yellow-green flowers. This grey-green plant has grooved stems. The leaves are narrow and fleshy. Look for rock samphire on cliffs on the south and west coasts of Britain.
Height: 15–30 cm
Flowers: June–August

DATE_____

PLACE_____

HABITAT_____

Heaths and Moors

Heaths and moors grow up in areas where forests have been cleared. They are open places with few trees to give protection from the wind. Large areas are often burned to encourage new growth – especially on grouse moors.

Heaths are found mainly in lowland areas. The soil is dry and sandy with a thin layer of peat. Moors are found in the north and west of Britain. They are much wetter than heaths and have a thick layer of peat.

Sometimes one kind of plant becomes much commoner than any other and takes over large areas of moorland. Look out for heather moors, bilberry moors and cotton-grass moors. The wettest parts may become a bog. Bright-green bog moss spreads over the water-logged soil and a different group of plants appears.

Gorse

GORSE and BROOM
In summer broom and gorse bushes add splashes of bright yellow to heathland. They have similar flowers and look alike from a distance. Close to they are easy to tell apart.

Gorse
The leaves are very sharp spines which cover the stems. Gorse also grows in grassy places and

DATE_____

PLACE_____

HABITAT_____

TORMENTIL

Tormentil looks rather like a buttercup but the flowers have only four petals, not five. The petals are heart-shaped. Look for the leaves which are divided into toothed segments, three large ones and two small ones.
Height: 5–50 cm
Flowers: May–October

DATE_____

PLACE_____

HABITAT_____

sometimes flowers all year round.
Height: up to 200 cm
Flowers: March–June

Broom

The leaves are divided into three leaflets. It grows in woods and waste places as well as on heathland, but never where the soil is chalky.
Height: up to 200 cm
Flowers: May–June

DATE_____

PLACE_____

HABITAT_____

BILBERRIES
Bilberry and its relatives can be found on almost any heath or moor. On high ground they may take over from other plants to form 'bilberry moors'.

Bilberry
A bushy plant with single pink bell-flowers. The black berries taste sweet. Bilberry also grows in woods with acid soil.
Height: up to 60 cm
Flowers: April–June

Bilberry

DATE_____

PLACE_____

HEATHERS
Heathers are very common on moors and heaths. When they flower whole areas look purple. Different kinds of heather grow on different parts of a moor or heath. Here are three common ones.

Heather
Heather or ling grows on almost any moor or heath. It has small purple flowers and pairs of tiny leaves.
Height: up to 60 cm
Flowers: August–September

Heather

DATE_____

PLACE_____

Cowberry

Cranberry

Cowberry
Cowberry looks like bilberry but has clusters of flowers and sour red berries. It grows on moors.
Height: up to 30 cm
Flowers: June–August

Cranberry
Sprawls along the ground in bogs and wet heaths. The flowers have curved petals. The berries are rather sour.
Height: up to 3 cm
Flowers: June–August

DATE_____

PLACE_____

DATE_____

PLACE_____

Bell-heather

Cross-leaved heath

Bell-heather
Bell-heather grows on the drier parts of moors and heaths. It has drooping, bell-shaped flowers with three leaves in each whorl.
Height: up to 60 cm.
Flowers: July–September

Cross-leaved heath
Cross-leaved heath grows on wet heaths and moors. It also has bell-shaped flowers with four leaves in each whorl.
Height: up to 60 cm
Flowers: July–September

DATE_____

PLACE_____

DATE_____

PLACE_____

HAREBELL
The blue, bell-shaped flowers hang on very fine stems. They sway and nod in the slightest breeze. Look for the pale, three-lobed style in the middle of the flower. Harebells are called bluebells in Scotland. They are also known as Old Man's bells and lady's thimbles.
Height: 15–40 cm
Flowers: July–September

DATE_____

PLACE_____

HABITAT_____

Flower-head

COTTON-GRASS
Cotton-grass has very narrow leaves and small **brown flower-heads**. It is hard to find until the white, fluffy seed-heads form. Then the boggy places where it grows seem to be covered in balls of cotton-wool.
Height: 20–60 cm
Flowers: May–June

DATE_____

PLACE_____

HABITAT_____

BOG ASPHODEL

This plant has very narrow leaves and spikes of yellow flowers. Each flower has six petals. Look for the six woolly stamens with orange anthers. Often large colonies grow in the wet hollows of bogs.
Height: 5–40 cm
Flowers: July–September

DATE_____

PLACE_____

HABITAT_____

ROUND-LEAVED SUNDEW

Sundews are bog plants. Look for the rosettes of leaves covered in sticky red hairs. When an insect becomes stuck to the hairs, the leaf rolls in over the insect and digests it. Afterwards the leaf unrolls. Upright stems carry small white flowers.
Height: 6–25 cm
Flowers: June–August

DATE_____

PLACE_____

HABITAT_____

Index

Bell-heather 45
Bilberries 44/45
Bindweed 36
Bitter vetch 18
Blackberry 16
Bluebell 14
Bog asphodel 47
Broom 43
Bugle 27
Bulbous buttercup 25
Bush vetch 18
Buttercups 22, 25

Chickweed 31, 33
Common field-speedwell 32
Common ragwort 39
Cottongrass 46
Cowberry 45
Cow parsley 20
Cranberry 45
Creeping buttercup 25
Creeping thistle 37
Cross-leaved heath 45
Cuckoo flower 29
Curled dock 26

Daisies 22, 24, 34/35
Dandelion 24
Dead-nettles 34/35
Dog's mercury 12

Feverfew 35
Field scabious 23
Foxglove 17
Fragrant orchid 29

Garlic mustard 21
Goosegrass 37
Gorse 42
Greater stitchwort 20

Hardheads 23
Harebell 46
Heathers 44/45
Herb robert 17
Horned poppy 39

Ivy 16

Lesser celandine 15
Lords and ladies 14

Marsh marigold 28
Meadow buttercup 25
Meadowsweet 22, 28

Nettles 31, 34/35

Ox-eye daisy 34

Primrose 15
Poppy 31

Ragged robin 26
Ramsons 13
Red campion 19
Red dead-nettle 35
Ribwort 22
Rock samphire 41
Rosebay willowherb 36
Round-leaved sundew 47

Scarlet pimpernel 32
Scentless mayweed 34
Sea holly 40
Sea rocket 40
Shepherd's purse 33
Sweet violet 19

Thrift 41
Tormentil 43
Traveller's joy 21
Tufted forget-me-not 30
Tufted vetch 18

Vetches 18
Viper's bugloss 38

Welted thistle 30
White clover 27
White dead-nettle 35
Wood anemone 13